loving repeating

A MUSICAL
ADAPTED
FROM THE
WRITINGS OF
GERTRUDE STEIN

---

loving repeating

Frank Galati

Northwestern University Press
Evanston, Illinois

Northwestern University Press
www.nupress.northwestern.edu

Printed in the United States of America

10   9   8   7   6   5   4   3   2   1

ISBN 978-0-8101-2005-1

Library of Congress Cataloging-in-Publication data are available from the
Library of Congress.

♾ The paper used in this publication meets the minimum requirements of the
American National Standard for Information Sciences—Permanence of Paper
for Printed Library Materials, ANSI Z39.48-1992.

for Peter Amster

CONTENTS

Production History

ix

Loving Repeating

1

Photographs

95

PRODUCTION HISTORY

Loving Repeating received its world premiere at the Museum of Contemporary Art in Chicago, February 14 to March 12, 2005, in a collaboration between About Face Theatre and the Museum of Contemporary Art. (An earlier version of the chamber musical was developed and presented at Northwestern University in 2002 under the title *A Long Gay Book*.) The eighty-minute show was performed with no intermission. It was directed by Frank Galati, with music by the composer Stephen Flaherty. The cast was as follows:

Gertrude Stein . . . . Cindy Gold

Young Gertrude . . . . Christine Mild

Alice B. Toklas. . . . . Jenny Powers

Chorus. . . . . . Zach Ford, Cristen Paige, Harriet Nzinga Plumpp, Travis Turner, and Bernie Yvon

A cast recording is available from Jay Records, featuring all the songs from the show.

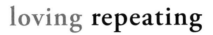
loving repeating

Gertrude Stein

Young Gertrude

Alice B. Toklas

Chorus:

Two Young Women
(Helen Furr and Georgine Skeene)

Three Young Men
(John, Paul, and Guy)

[Gertrude Stein, age 60, speaks from a lectern at the University of Chicago, November 1934.]

GERTRUDE:

I am going to read what I have written to read because in a general way it is easier even if it is not better and in a general way it is better even if it is not easier to read what has been written than to say what has not been written. Any way that is one way to feel about it.

To begin with, I seem always to be doing the talking when I am any where but in spite of that I do listen. I always listen. I always have listened. I always have listened to the way everybody has to tell what they have to say. In other words I always have listened in my way of listening until they have told me and told me until I really know it, that is know what they are.

I cannot remember not talking all the time and all the same feeling that while I was talking while I was seeing that I was not only hearing but seeing while I was talking and that at the same time the relation between myself knowing I was talking and those to whom I was talking and incidentally to whom I was listening were coming to tell me and tell me in their way every thing that made them.

And then I went to college . . .

[*Music.*]

and there for a little while I was tremendously occupied with finding out what was inside myself to make me what I was. I think that does happen to one at that time. It had been happening before going to college but going to college made it more lively. And being so occupied with what made me myself inside me, made me perhaps not stop talking but for awhile it made me stop listening.

At any rate that is the way it seems to me now looking back at it.

[*Gertrude sees herself
as a college student.*]

YOUNG GERTRUDE
[*singing*]:

I SPY A FLY.
IT WAS A BEE.
YOU ARE MY HONEY HONEY SUCKLE.
I AM YOUR BEE.
YOU ARE MY HONEY HONEY SUCKLE.
I AM YOUR BEE.

COME ALONG AND SIT TO ME
SIT WITH ME
SIT BY ME,
COME ALONG AND SIT WITH ME
ALL THE NEXT DAY TOO.

A SONATINA SONG
IS JUST THIS LONG.
A SONATINA LONG
IS JUST THIS SONG.

COME ALONG AND SIT WITH ME
SIT BY ME SIT FOR ME,
COME ALONG AND SIT BY ME
SIT BY ME AND SEE.

SENECA SAID
THAT HE LOVED TO BE WED.
AND HE SAID
THAT WAS WHAT
HE SAID.

CAREFULLY
MEDDLE WITH ME.
DO NOT BE PLAINTIVE AND SING,
MEDDLE WITH ME,
MEDDLE WITH ME,
MEDAL,
WHO HAS THE MEDAL.
SING REASONABLY.

COME ALONG AND SIT WITH ME,
SIT BY ME SIT FOR ME,
COME ALONG AND SIT BY ME,
SIT BY ME AND SEE.
SIT BY ME AND SEE.

GERTRUDE:

While I was at college and doing philosophy and
psychology I became more and more interested in my
own mental and physical processes and less in that
of others and all I then was learning of what made
people what they were came to me by experience and
not by talking and listening.

[*Young Gertrude and Two Young Women dance.*]

TWO YOUNG WOMEN AND YOUNG GERTRUDE:

AH!
COME ALONG AND SIT BY ME
SIT BY ME AND SEE

GERTRUDE:

Then as I say I became more interested in psychology,
and one of the things I did was testing reactions

of the average college student in a state of normal activity and in the state of fatigue induced by their examinations.

YOUNG GERTRUDE
[*to Gertrude*]:

I was supposed to be interested in their reactions but soon I found that I was not but instead that I was enormously interested in the types of their characters.

GERTRUDE:

That is what I even then thought of as the bottom nature of them, and when in May 1898 I wrote my half of the report of these experiments I expressed these results as follows:

YOUNG GERTRUDE
[*taking Gertrude's place
at the lectern*]:

In these descriptions it will be readily observed that habits of attention are reflexes of the complete character of the individual.

GERTRUDE:

Then that was over . . .

> [*Young Gertrude leaves the lectern
> and joins the Two Young Women
> and Three Young Men. They dance.*]

YOUNG GERTRUDE

AND CHORUS:

COME ALONG AND SIT BY ME
SIT BY ME AND SING!

GERTRUDE:

. . . and I went to the medical school where I
was bored and where once more myself and my
experiences were more actively interesting me than
the life inside of others.

YOUNG GERTRUDE:

But then after that once more I began to listen,

GERTRUDE:

I had left the medical school and I had for the
moment nothing to do

YOUNG GERTRUDE:

nothing to do but talk and look and listen,

GERTRUDE:

and this I did tremendously.

YOUNG GERTRUDE:

I then began again to think about the bottom nature
in people,

GERTRUDE:

I began to get enormously interested in hearing
how everybody said the same thing over and over
again

YOUNG GERTRUDE:

over and over again with infinite variations but
over and over again until finally if you listened
with great intensity you could hear it rise and
fall and tell all that that there was inside
them,

GERTRUDE:

not so much by the actual words they said

YOUNG GERTRUDE:

or the thoughts they had

GERTRUDE:

but the movement of their thoughts and
words endlessly the same and endlessly
different.

YOUNG GERTRUDE AND CHORUS
[*singing*]:

LOVING REPEATING IS ONE WAY OF BEING.
REPEATING IS ALWAYS IN ALL OF THEM.
REPEATING IN THEM COMES OUT OF THEM,
SLOWLY MAKING CLEAR TO ANYONE THAT
   LOOKS CLOSELY AT THEM
THE NATURE AND THE NATURES MIXED UP
   IN THEM.
THIS SOMETIME COMES TO BE CLEAR

WOMEN:

IN EVERY ONE.

MEN:

IN EVERYONE.

ALL:

EVERYONE!

REPEATING IS A WONDERFUL THING IN
   LIVING BEING.
SOMETIME THEN THE NATURE OF EVERY ONE
COMES TO BE CLEAR TO SOMEONE LISTENING
TO THE REPEATING COMING OUT OF EACH ONE.

WOMEN:

MEN:

LOVING REPEATING.
LOVING REPEATING.   LOVING REPEATING.
LOVING REPEATING.   LOVING REPEATING.
                      LOVING REPEATING.

ALL:

LOVING REPEATING.

YOUNG GERTRUDE
[*singing*]:

THERE ARE MANY THAT I KNOW
AND THEY KNOW IT.
THEY ARE ALL OF THEM REPEATING
AND I HEAR IT.
MORE AND MORE I UNDERSTAND IT.
I LOVE IT AND I TELL IT.
I LOVE IT AND ALWAYS I WILL TELL IT.

CHORUS:

LOVING REPEATING.
LOVING REPEATING IS ONE WAY OF BEING.

YOUNG GERTRUDE:

THEY LIVE IT AND I SEE IT AND I HEAR IT
THEY REPEAT IT AND I HEAR IT AND I SEE IT,
SOMETIMES THEN ALWAYS I UNDERSTAND IT,
SOMETIMES THEN ALWAYS THERE IS A
COMPLETED HISTORY OF EACH ONE BY IT,
SOMETIME THEN I WILL TELL THE COMPLETED
HISTORY OF EACH ONE
AS BY REPEATING I COME TO KNOW . . .

CHORUS:

AS BY REPEATING I COME TO KNOW . . .

YOUNG GERTRUDE:

AS BY REPEATING

YOUNG GERTRUDE AND CHORUS:

I COME TO KNOW

YOUNG GERTRUDE:

I COME TO KNOW IT.

CHORUS:

LOVING REPEATING.
LOVING REPEATING IS ONE WAY OF BEING.

*[A "spoken"
dance break
follows.*

*The Chorus
speaks the text
in variation as
Young Gertrude
sings over.*

*Gertrude speaks
in her own
rhythm over
the others.]*

WOMEN AND MEN:

Loving repeating
Is one way of being.
Repeating is always
In all of them.
Loving repeating
Is one way of being.
Repeating is always
In all of them.
Loving repeating
Is one way of being
Repeating is always
In all of them.
Loving repeating
Is one way of being.
Repeating is always,
Repeating is always,
REPEATING!

YOUNG GERTRUDE:

LOVING REPEATING!

REPEATING IS ALWAYS
IN ALL OF THEM!

LOVING REPEATING
IS ONE WAY OF BEING.
REPEATING IS ALWAYS
REPEATING IS ALWAYS
REPEATING!

GERTRUDE:

Loving repeating
Is one way of being.

Repeating is
Always in all of them.

Loving repeating
is one way of being.

Repeating is always
in all of them.

YOUNG GERTRUDE:

THEY LIVE IT AND I SEE IT AND I HEAR IT

CHORUS:

THEY LIVE IT AND I HEAR IT

15

YOUNG GERTRUDE:

THEY REPEAT IT AND I HEAR IT AND I SEE IT.

CHORUS:

I SEE IT AND I HEAR IT.
SHOOP!

YOUNG GERTRUDE:

SOMETIMES THEN ALWAYS I UNDERSTAND IT,

CHORUS:

I COME TO KNOW . . .

YOUNG GERTRUDE:

SOMETIMES THEN ALWAYS THERE IS A
COMPLETED HISTORY OF EACH ONE BY IT,

CHORUS:

I COME TO KNOW . . .

YOUNG GERTRUDE:

SOMETIME THEN I WILL TELL

YOUNG GERTRUDE
AND CHORUS:

THE COMPLETED HISTORY
OF EACH ONE

YOUNG GERTRUDE:

AS BY REPEATING I COME TO KNOW . . .

CHORUS:

AS BY REPEATING I COME TO KNOW . . .

YOUNG GERTRUDE:

AS BY REPEATING

YOUNG GERTRUDE AND CHORUS:

I COME TO KNOW

YOUNG GERTRUDE:

I COME TO KNOW IT.

CHORUS:

LOVING REPEATING.
LOVING REPEATING IS ONE WAY OF BEING.

YOUNG GERTRUDE:

I COME TO KNOW IT.

CHORUS:

LOVING REPEATING.
LOVING REPEATING.

[*Young Gertrude and the Chorus
now sing together in full harmony,
their voices unaccompanied.*]

YOUNG GERTRUDE AND CHORUS:

I COME TO KNOW . . .
IT.

YOUNG GERTRUDE AND ENSEMBLE:

EVERY ONE ALWAYS IS REPEATING THE WHOLE
     OF THEM.
EVERY ONE IS REPEATING THE WHOLE OF THEM,
SUCH REPEATING IS THEN ALWAYS IN THEM
AND SO SOMETIME SOME ONE WHO SEES THEM
WILL HAVE A COMPLETE UNDERSTANDING
OF THE WHOLE OF EACH ONE OF THEM,
WILL HAVE A COMPLETED HISTORY OF EVERY MAN
     AND EVERY WOMAN
THEY EVER COME TO KNOW IN THEIR
     LIVING,
EVERY MAN AND EVERY WOMAN WHO WERE
OR ARE OR WILL BE LIVING
WHOM SUCH A ONE CAN COME TO KNOW
IN LIVING.
THIS THEN IS A HISTORY OF MANY MEN AND
     WOMEN,
SOMETIME THERE WILL BE A HISTORY
OF . . . ONE.

YOUNG GERTRUDE:

ONE.

[*Alice B. Toklas, age 30, steps into a shaft of light.
She and Young Gertrude see each other.
A bell rings.*]

ALICE
[*singing*]:

I SPY A FLY.
IT WAS A BEE.
YOU ARE MY HONEY HONEY SUCKLE.
I AM YOUR BEE.
YOU ARE MY HONEY HONEY SUCKLE.
I AM YOUR BEE.

[*Young Gertrude sits at a small table set for tea.*]

GERTRUDE
[*speaking*]:

I caught sight of a splendid Misses. She had
handkerchiefs and kisses. She had eyes and yellow
shoes she had everything to choose and she chose me.

In passing through France she wore a Chinese hat and so did I. In looking at the sun she read a map. And so did I. In eating fish and pork she just grew fat. And so did I. In loving a blue sea she had a pain. And so did I. In loving me she of necessity thought first. And so did I. How prettily we swim. Not in water. Not on land. But in love.

YOUNG GERTRUDE
[*singing*]:

IN LOVE . . .
COME ALONG AND SIT TO ME
SIT WITH ME
SIT BY ME,
COME ALONG AND SIT WITH ME
ALL THE NEXT DAY TOO.

YOUNG GERTRUDE AND ALICE
[*singing*]:

ALL THE NEXT DAY
TOO.

[*Young Gertrude and Alice vocalize in close harmony, unaccompanied.*]

YOUNG GERTRUDE AND ALICE
[*singing*]:

TWO . . .
TWO . . .
TWO!!

[*The music segues grandly as a sign descends
from above: Paris, 27, rue de Fleurus, 1907.*]

YOUNG GERTRUDE AND ALICE:

TWO!!

CHORUS:

TWO!!

GERTRUDE:

"A Lyrical Opera Made By Two" To Be Sung.

CHORUS
[*singing*]:

LA-LA-LA-LA-LA!

A LYRICAL OPERA MADE BY TWO

A LYRICAL OPERA MADE BY TWO

MEN OF THE CHORUS:

MADE BY TWO, MADE BY MADE BY TWO

ALL:

TO BE SUNG
SUNG
TO BE SUNG
SUNG
TO BE SUNG!
TO BE SUNG!

LA-LA-LA-LA-LA!

GERTRUDE:

Setting:
A large lofty room cut by rows of pictures . . .

[As Gertrude describes the room
it is set up around Young Gertrude
and Alice. Paintings descend,
furniture is brought on.]

GERTRUDE:

. . . and in the middle corner a work-table round with
drawers in the shape of a Maltese cross and on it a seal
red small medium sized bull a tortoise shell lamp and
a glass of tiny hyacinths fresh flowers and on either
side one side a small arm chair with a large medium
sized pleasant handsome man . . .

[*Young Gertrude sits.*]

GERTRUDE:

. . . and on the other side a large arm chair chintz
covered with a fair sized dark charming medium
sized lady.

[*Alice sits.*]

YOUNG GERTRUDE
[*singing*]:

MY WIFE IS MY LIFE
IS MY LIFE IS MY WIFE
IS MY WIFE IS MY LIFE
IS MY LIFE IS MY WIFE
IS MY LIFE
IS MY WIFE

ALICE:

NODS ONCE IN AGREEMENT

YOUNG GERTRUDE:

MY WIFE IS MY LIFE
IS MY LIFE IS MY WIFE
IS MY WIFE IS MY LIFE
IS MY LIFE IS MY WIFE
IS MY LIFE
IS MY WIFE

ALICE:

NODS ONCE IN AGREEMENT

YOUNG GERTRUDE:

MY WIFE IS MY LIFE
IS MY LIFE IS MY WIFE
IS MY WIFE
IS MY LIFE
IS MY LIFE
IS MY WIFE
IS MY LIFE

MY WIFE IS MY LIFE
IS MY LIFE IS MY WIFE
IS MY WIFE IS MY LIFE
IS MY LIFE IS MY WIFE
IS MY LIFE
IS MY WIFE.

ALICE:

NODS ONCE

YOUNG GERTRUDE:

IS MY LIFE

ALICE:

NODS ONCE IN AGREEMENT

YOUNG GERTRUDE:

A Lyric.

GERTRUDE:

Scene Two.

TWO YOUNG WOMEN:

LA-LA-LA-LA-LA-LA
LA-LA-LA-LA-LA
LA-LA-LA-LA-LA

YOUNG GERTRUDE:

COME FIRE FLY
AND LIGHT UP BABY'S NOSE
COME FIRE FLY
AND LIGHT UP BABY'S NOSE

ALICE:

COME FIRE FLY
AND LIGHT UP BABY'S
NOSE

YOUNG GERTRUDE, ALICE:

COME FIRE FLY

YOUNG GERTRUDE, TWO YOUNG WOMEN:

AND LIGHT UP BABY'S NOSE

ALICE:

IN THE VILLA BARDI AT FLORENCE
A TALL PROPRIETOR CALLING
TO HIS WORKMAN
PAOLO.

TWO YOUNG WOMEN:

LA-LA-LA-LA
LA-LA-LA-LA

GERTRUDE:

Seated Large Medium Sized Pleasant Handsome
Man also seated Fair sized dark charming medium
sized lady.

YOUNG GERTRUDE:

A CUCKOO BIRD IS SITTING ON A CUCKOO TREE
SINGING TO ME
OH SINGING TO ME.

YOUNG GERTRUDE:	ALICE:
TO ME	A CUCKOO BIRD
	IS SITTING
OH	ON A CUCKOO TREE

YOUNG GERTRUDE AND ALICE:

SINGING TO ME
OH SINGING TO ME

TWO YOUNG WOMEN:

AH AH . . .

YOUNG GERTRUDE:

A ROCKY UNDULATING ROAD SIDE
SMALL ORCHIDS GROWING
NOT ABUNDANTLY
AND SOME LAVENDER.

TWO YOUNG WOMEN:

LA-LA-LA-LA
LA-LA-LA-LA

YOUNG GERTRUDE AND ALICE:	TWO YOUNG WOMEN:
TWO WALKING	
	LA-LA-LA-LA
TWO WALKING	
	LA-LA-LA-LA
TWO WALKING	
	LA-LA-LA-LA
TWO WALKING	
	LA-LA-LA-LA.

YOUNG GERTRUDE:

JOHN QUILLY JOHN QUILLY
MY BABE BABY
IS SWEETER
THAN EVEN JOHN QUILLIES ARE.

ALICE
[*speaking*]:

Hesitation in memory does not make it difficulty to
be disturbed.

YOUNG GERTRUDE:

JOHN QUILLY JOHN QUILLY
MY BABE BABY
IS SWEETER
THAN EVEN JOHN QUILLIES ARE

TWO YOUNG WOMEN:

LA-LA-LA-LA-LA

ALICE
[*speaking*]:

Before this it is a preparation to make a fountain.

YOUNG GERTRUDE:

Being afterward.

ALICE:

Uno due tre quattro cinque se uno due tre quattro.

YOUNG GERTRUDE:

The palace of Louis XIV known as Versailles.

ALICE:

To have a guide will you have a guide no guide inside inside no guide.

YOUNG GERTRUDE:

Back to back in the presence of a fact.

ALICE:

Very nice and quiet I thank you.

YOUNG GERTRUDE:

A lyric when they have met.

GERTRUDE:

Scene Three:

YOUNG GERTRUDE:

Sing softly caramel.

ALICE
[*singing*]:

A COW WILL BE A LARGE AND LOOSE CARAMEL
A COW WILL BE A LARGE
A LARGE AND LOOSE CARAMEL.
AND WILL BE WELL.
AND WILL BE WELL.

A CARAMEL.

A COW IT WILL BE HOW
A LARGE A LOOSE A COW
LET IT LET IT PET IT
GET IT SET IT.
A COW HOW LARGE
AND LOOSE CARAMEL
JUST AS WELL CARAMEL.

[*scatting*]

Ba da un ba da un ba da un
CARAMEL

GERTRUDE
[*spoken*]:

Scene Four:

ALICE
[*singing*]:

SHE SITTING.

YOUNG GERTRUDE:

A COW COMING.

ALICE:

HE WELCOMING

BOTH:

A COW COMING . . .

[*Sound effect: a cow mooing.*]

ALICE:

A COW HAS COME HE IS PLEASED
AND SHE IS CONTENT
AS A COW
CAME AND WENT.
HE AND SHE AND SENT.

YOUNG GERTRUDE:

SO NICELY.

ALICE:

TO MEAN TO MEAN   YOUNG GERTRUDE:
THAT THEY ADVERTISE
AN ODORLESS JASMINE.   AN ODORLESS
                                 JASMINE.
JASMINE   AN ODORLESS JASMINE

HMM   HMM

BOTH:

HMM

OPERA CHORUS:

HMM!!!

CHORUS WOMEN:

CHORUS MEN:

LA LA LA LA LA
LA LA LA LA
LA LA LA LA LA LA
LA L A LA L A
LA LA LA

LA LA LA
LA LA LA
LA LA LA LA
LA LA LA

CHORUS:

A LYRICAL OPERA
MADE BY TWO
TO BE SUNG!

GERTRUDE:

"A Lyrical Opera":
Finale!

YOUNG GERTRUDE:

AND NOW A LITTLE SCENE WITH A QUEEN
CONTENTED BY THE COW WHICH HAS COME

ALICE AND THE OPERA CHORUS:

WHICH HAS COME

YOUNG GERTRUDE, ALICE, AND THE OPERA CHORUS:

YES, THE COW HAS COME!
AND BEEN SENT AND BEEN SEEN.
A DEAR
DEAREST QUEEN.

SOPRANO SOLO:

HA HA!

YOUNG GERTRUDE, ALICE, AND THE OPERA CHORUS:

AND BEEN SENT AND BEEN SEEN.
A DEAR
DEAREST QUEEN.

SOPRANO SOLO:

HA HA!

CHORUS GROUP 1	CHORUS GROUP 2	CHORUS GROUP 3
A LYRICAL OPERA	A LYRICAL OPERA	
AN OPERA		A LYRICAL OPERA

YOUNG GERTRUDE, ALICE, AND CHORUS:

A LYRICAL OPERA MADE BY TWO
TO BE SUNG!
TO BE SUNG!
TO BE SUNG!
SUNG!
SUNG!
SUNG!
SUNG!!!

GERTRUDE:

CURTAIN!

[*speaking*]:

When I was at a dinner party at Beverly Hills in
Hollywood, there were a great many of the big
vedettes of the cinema. After dinner all these people
were seated in front of me, and I did not know what
it was all about or what they wanted, and finally one
blurted out, "What we want to know is how do you
get so much publicity?"

So I told them, "By having such a small audience. Begin with a small audience. If that audience really believes, they make a big noise."

They thought about that and then another one blurted out, "Miss Stein, why don't you write the way you talk?'

And I said, "Why don't you read the way I write?"

[*Young Gertrude sits at a typewriter and types.*
Gertrude passes Alice a sealed envelope.
She moves into a golden light and slowly opens it.
Young Gertrude continues to type.]

CHORUS
[*singing*]:

KISS MY LIPS SHE DID
KISS MY LIPS AGAIN SHE DID
KISS MY LIPS OVER AND OVER AGAIN
SHE DID.

MRS. MISSES KISSES MRS. MOST MRS.
MISSES KISSES MISSES KISSES
MOST.

[Music continues under.]

GERTRUDE
[speaking]:

He stopped to stoop and say
Nellie and Lillie
Lillie and Nellie
Nellie and Lillie
Not Lillie
Not Lillie and Nellie
Not Nellie Not Lillie
Not any Lillie
Not any Nellie
Very well and very bell.
What is a door just shut is a door more and more.
Little Alice B. is the wife for me.
Little Alice B. so tenderly is born
So long so she can be borne along by a husband strong
who has not his hair shorn. And what size is wise. The
right size is nice. How can you credit me with wishes.
I wish you a very happy birthday.
One two, one two I come to you. Today there is
nothing but the humble expression of a husband's
love. Take it.

CAN WE EAT TO-DAY,
TO-DAY IS THE MONTH OF MAY,
CAN WE EAT TO-DAY
LARGELY.

AND HOW NICELY WE SING
OF THE THIRTEENTH OF APRIL.
THE THIRTEENTH OF APRIL
IS THE DAY
WHICH IS THE MONTH OF MAY.
ON THAT DAY WE HESITATE TO SING.
WHY BECAUSE WE ARE SO HAPPILY
FLOURISHING.

WE MAKE A LIST,

WOMAN ONE:

A SAUCE DISH,

MAN ONE:

A SAUCER,

MAN TWO:

A TILE,

MAN THREE:

A GILDED CUSHION,

WOMAN TWO:

A HANDKERCHIEF,

MAN ONE:

A GLASS,

YOUNG GERTRUDE AND ALICE:

TWO PLATES

ALL:

AND AN ORATORY.
AND WHAT DO WE DO
IN THE ORATORY.
WE TELL ABOUT OUR BLESSINGS.

WE BLESS THE DAY
EVERY DAY.

EVERY DAY.
EVERY DAY.

EVERY DAY.
EVERY DAY!

[*Rhythm break. They dance.*]

ALL:

EVERY DAY.
EVERY DAY.

YOUNG GERTRUDE:	ALICE:	MEN [*echoing*]:
EVERY DAY.	CAN WE EAT TODAY,	
		WOMEN TODAY IS THE MONTH OF MAY,
EVERY DAY	CAN WE EAT	CAN WE EAT
TODAY . . .	TODAY . . .	TODAY . . .

ALL:

TODAY!

[*Light guitar accompanies
the following.*]

GERTRUDE
[*speaking*]:

We say gayly the troubadour plays his guitar to
his star.

How often do we need trees and hills. Not often.
And how often do we need mountains.

ALICE
[*speaking*]:

Not very often.

GERTRUDE:

And how often do we need birds.

ALICE:

Not often.

GERTRUDE:

And how often do we need wishes.

ALICE:

Not often.

[*Alice removes her glasses.*]

And how often do we need glasses not often.

GERTRUDE:

We drink wine and we make, well we have not made it yet.

ALICE:

How often do we need a kiss.

GERTRUDE:

Very often and we add when tenderness overwhelms us we speedily eat veal. And what else, ham and a little pork

ALICE:

and raw artichokes and ripe olives

GERTRUDE:

and chester cheese and cakes and caramels and all the melon.

ALICE:

We still have a great deal of it left. I wonder where it is. Conserved melon. Let me offer it to you.

GERTRUDE:

How can you sleep so sweetly, how can you be so very well.

YOUNG GERTRUDE
[*speaking*]:

Very well.

GERTRUDE
[*speaking*]:

Maestro!

[*A musical fanfare as the curtains part
and Three Young Men leap from
the wings into a spot light.*]

GERTRUDE
[*speaking*]:

As a wife has a cow.

A Love Story.

MAN TWO
[*speaking*]:

Nearly all of it to be as a wife has a cow, a love story.

MAN ONE
[*speaking*]:

All of it to be as a wife has a cow,

MAN THREE
[*speaking*]:

all of it to be as a wife has a cow, a love story.

THREE YOUNG MEN
[*singing*]:

AS TO BE ALL OF IT
AS TO BE A WIFE
AS A WIFE HAS A COW,
A LOVE STORY,
ALL OF IT
AS TO BE ALL OF IT
AS A WIFE
ALL OF IT
AS TO BE
AS A WIFE HAS A COW
A LOVE STORY.

[*Vaudeville sound effect: cow moo.*]

HAS MADE,
AS IT HAS MADE
AS IT HAS MADE,
HAS MADE HAS TO BE
AS A WIFE HAS A COW,
A LOVE STORY.

[*Vaudeville sound effect: cow moo.*]

HAS MADE AS TO BE
AS A WIFE HAS A COW
A LOVE STORY.
AS A WIFE HAS A COW,
HAS A COW AS NOW
A LOVE STORY.

HAS TO BE
AS A WIFE HAS A COW
A LOVE STORY.

HAS MADE AS TO BE
AS A WIFE HAS A COW
A LOVE STORY.
LOVE STORY.

WHEN HE CAN,
AND FOR THAT
WHEN HE CAN,
FOR THAT.
WHEN HE CAN,
AND FOR THAT

MAN THREE:

WHEN HE CAN

MAN ONE AND MAN TWO:

FOR THAT

THREE YOUNG MEN:

WHEN HE CAN.
FOR THAT
WHEN HE CAN.
FOR THAT.
AND WHEN HE CAN
AND FOR THAT.
OR THAT,

MAN THREE:

AND WHEN HE CAN.

MAN ONE AND MAN TWO:

FOR THAT,

ALL:

AND WHEN HE CAN.

MAN THREE:

AND WHEN HE CAN.

MAN ONE AND MAN TWO:

FOR THAT,

ALL:

AND WHEN HE CAN.

[*Vaudeville music continues under.*]

MAN TWO
[*speaking*]:

And to in six and another. And to and in and six and
another. And to and in and six and another. And to
in six and and to and in and six and another. And to
and in and six and another. And to and six and in and
another and and to and six and another and and to
and in and six and and to and six and in and another.

MAN ONE
[*speaking*]:

In came in there, came in there come out of there.
In came in come out of there. Come out there in
came in there. Come out of there and in and come
out of there. Came in there, come out of there.

MAN THREE:

Feeling or for it, as feeling or for it,

MAN ONE:

came in or come in, or come out of there

MAN THREE:

or feeling as feeling as feeling as for it.

MAN TWO
[*in vaudeville rhythm*]:

As a wife has a cow.

MAN ONE:

Came in and come out.

THREE YOUNG MEN:

As a wife has a cow

[*sung*]

A LOVE STORY

[*Instrumental (dance) break.
A cubist vaudeville cow enters and
dances with the Three Young Men.*]

THREE YOUNG MEN:

A LOVE STORY

MAN ONE:

Not and now, now and not, not and now, by and by
not and now, as not, as soon as not not and now, now
as soon now now as soon, now as soon as soon as
now. Just as soon just now just now just as soon just
as soon as now. Just as soon as now.

*[Gertrude enters
on a cow bicycle.]*

GERTRUDE
[speaking]:

Loving repeating is one way of being. Loving
repeating is in a way earth feeling. In some it is
repeating that gives to them always a solid feeling
of being. In some children there is more feeling in
repeating eating and playing, in some in story-telling
and their feeling. Loving repeating then in some is
their natural way of complete being.

*[Two Young Women
(Helen and Georgine)
pop out of the cow costume.]*

GERTRUDE:

Loving repeating

TWO YOUNG WOMEN:

Loving repeating

GERTRUDE AND TWO YOUNG WOMEN:

Loving repeating

TWO YOUNG WOMEN:

MMM.

GERTRUDE:

Loving repeating

TWO YOUNG WOMEN:	GERTRUDE [*in rhythm*]:
DO THEY AS THEY DO SO.	As they do so
AND DO THEY DO SO.	Do they do so
WE FEEL WE FEEL. WE FEEL OR IF WE FEEL IF WE FEEL OR IF WE FEEL. WE FEEL OR IF WE FEEL.	As they do so
AS IT IS MADE MADE A DAY MADE A DAY OR TWO MADE A DAY,	Do they do so
AS IT IS MADE A DAY OR TWO, AS IT IS MADE A DAY.	Loving repeating Loving repeating
MADE A DAY. MADE A DAY. NOT AWAY A DAY. BY DAY.	Not away a day. By day. As it is made
AS IT IS MADE	
AS IT IS MADE	As it is made

GERTRUDE AND TWO YOUNG WOMEN:

AS IT IS MADE
A DAY.
Made a day.
On the fifteenth of November as they say, said
Anyway.

[*Gertrude steps forward.*]

GERTRUDE
[*speaking*]:

One day, November fifteenth to be exact, the doorbell
rang and in walked Lady Rothermere and T. S. Eliot.
He and I had a solemn conversation, mostly about
split infinitives and other grammatical solecisms, and
why I use them. Finally they rose to go and Eliot said
that if he printed anything of mine in *The Criterion* it
would have to be my very latest thing. They left and
I began to write a portrait of T. S. Eliot and called it
the fifteenth of November, that being this day and
so there could be no doubt but that it was my latest
thing. It was all about wool is wool and silk is silk or
wool is woolen and silk is silken. I sent it to T. S. Eliot
and he accepted it but, naturally, he did not print it.

Then in early spring there was a note from *The Criterion* asking would Miss Stein mind if her contribution appeared in the October number. I replied:

Nothing could be more suitable than the fifteenth of November on the fifteenth of October.

ALL

[singing]:

ON THE FIFTEENTH OF OCTOBER
AS THEY SAY,
SAID ANYWAY,
WHAT IS IT AS THEY EXPECT,
AS THEY EXPECT IT
OR AS THEY EXPECTED IT,
AS THEY EXPECT IT
AND AS THEY EXPECTED IT,
EXPECT IT OR FOR IT,
EXPECTED IT
AND IT IS EXPECTED OF IT.
AS THEY SAY SAID ANYWAY.
WHAT IS IT THEY EXPECT FOR IT,
WHAT IS IT AND IT IS
AS THEY EXPECT OF IT.

WHAT IS IT.
WHAT IS IT
WHAT IS IT
WHAT IS IT
WHAT IS IT
WHAT IS IT

THE FIFTEENTH OF OCTOBER
AS THEY SAY
AS THEY EXPECT
OR AS THEY EXPECTED ´
AS THEY EXPECT FOR IT.
WHAT IS IT
WHAT IS IT
WHAT IS IT
WHAT IS IT
WHAT IS IT
WHAT IS IT
THE FIFTEENTH OF OCTOBER
AS THEY SAY
AND AS EXPECTED OF IT,
THE FIFTEENTH OF OCTOBER
AS THEY SAY,
WHAT IS IT

WOMAN ONE:

AS EXPECTED OF IT.

OTHERS:

WHAT IS IT
AND THE FIFTEENTH OF OCTOBER
AS THEY SAY
THE FIFTEENTH OF OCTOBER.

YOUNG GERTRUDE, ALICE, AND CHORUS
[*singing*]:

AND MY WIFE HAS A COW AS NOW,
MY WIFE HAS A COW

YOUNG GERTRUDE AND ALICE:

A LOVE STORY.

CHORUS:

MY WIFE HAS A COW,
HAS A COW AS NOW

YOUNG GERTRUDE AND ALICE:

A LOVE STORY.

CHORUS:

HAVING, HAVING A COW

YOUNG GERTRUDE AND ALICE:

A LOVE STORY

CHORUS:

AND HAVING COW NOW,
MY WIFE HAS A COW

YOUNG GERTRUDE, ALICE, AND CHORUS:

AND NOW.
MY WIFE HAS A COW!!

[*Vaudeville sound effect: cow moo.
The curtain falls.*]

GERTRUDE
[*speaking*]:

Now listen! Can't you see that when the language was
new—as it was with Chaucer and Homer—the poet
could use the name of a thing and the thing was really

there? He could say "O moon," "O sea," "O love," and the moon and the sea and love were really there. And can't you see that after hundreds of years had gone by and thousands of poems had been written, he could call on those words and find that they were just wornout literary words? The excitingness of pure being had withdrawn from them; they were just rather stale literary words. Now the poet has to work in the excitingness of pure being; he has to get back that intensity into the language. We all know that it's hard to write poetry in a late age; and we know that you have to put some strangeness something unexpected, into the structure of the sentence in order to bring back vitality to the noun. Now it's not enough to be bizarre; the strangeness in the sentence structure has to come from the poetic gift, too. That's why it's doubly hard to be a poet in a late age. Now you all have seen hundreds of poems about roses and you know in your bones the rose is not there. All those songs that sopranos sing as encores about "I have a garden; oh what a garden!" Now I don't want to put too much emphasis on that line, because it's just one line in a longer poem. But I notice that you all know it; you make fun of it, but you know it. Now listen! I'm no fool. I know that in daily life we don't go around saying "is a . . . [rose] is a . . . [rose] . . . is a . . ." Yes, I'm no fool; but I think that in that line the rose is red for the first time in English poetry for a hundred years.

[A curtain opens to reveal
Young Gertrude and Alice, now in middle age.
They hold hands and slowly face forward.]

YOUNG GERTRUDE AND ALICE
[singing]:

KISS MY LIPS SHE DID
KISS MY LIPS AGAIN SHE DID
KISS MY LIPS OVER AND OVER AGAIN

[Young Gertrude and Alice kiss.]

YOUNG GERTRUDE AND ALICE:

SHE DID.

GERTRUDE:

Miss Furr

[Young Gertrude turns and escorts
Helen Furr (Woman One) onto the stage.
Miss Furr is dressed exactly
like the Young Gertrude.]

GERTRUDE:

And Miss Skeene.

[*Alice turns and escorts Georgine Skeene (Woman Two) onto the stage. Miss Skeene is dressed exactly like Alice.*]

GERTRUDE
[*speaking*]:

Helen Furr had quite a pleasant voice a voice quite worth cultivating. She did not mind working. She worked to cultivate her voice. She did not find it gay living in the same place where she had always been living. She went to a place where some were cultivating something, voices and other things needing cultivating.

She met Georgine Skeene there who was cultivating her voice which some thought was quite a pleasant one.

YOUNG GERTRUDE AND ALICE
[*singing*]:

AH

HELEN AND GEORGINE
[*singing*]:

AH

ALL FOUR WOMEN:

AH!

YOUNG GERTRUDE:

Helen Furr and Georgine Skeene lived together then.

ALICE:

Georgine Skeene liked traveling.

YOUNG GERTRUDE:

Helen Furr did not care about traveling, she liked to stay in one place and be gay there.

HELEN AND GEORGINE:

They were together then and traveled to another place and stayed there and were gay there.

HELEN AND GEORGINE
[*singing*]:

THEY STAYED THERE
AND WERE GAY THERE,
NOT VERY GAY THERE,

YOUNG GERTRUDE AND ALICE:

JUST GAY THERE.

HELEN AND GEORGINE:

THEY WERE

ALL FOUR WOMEN:

BOTH GAY THERE,

HELEN AND GEORGINE:

THEY WERE REGULARLY WORKING THERE

YOUNG GERTRUDE AND ALICE:

BOTH OF THEM

ALL FOUR WOMEN:

CULTIVATING THEIR VOICES THERE,

[*Helen and Georgine vocalize together in close harmony.*]

HELEN AND GEORGINE:

AH
AH!!

GEORGINE:

AH!

HELEN:

HA-HA-HA!

GEORGINE:

AH!

HELEN:

HA-HA-HA!

BOTH:

HA!

GEORGINE:

GEORGINE SKEENE WAS GAY THERE
AND SHE WAS REGULAR,
REGULAR IN BEING GAY,
REGULAR IN NOT BEING GAY,
REGULAR IN BEING A GAY ONE
WHO WAS ONE NOT BEING GAY
HMM . . .
LONGER THAN WAS NEEDED
TO BE ONE
BEING QUITE A GAY ONE.

HELEN AND GEORGINE:

THEY WERE BOTH GAY THEN THERE
AND BOTH WORKING THERE THEN.
THEY WERE IN A WAY
BOTH GAY THERE
WHERE THERE WERE MANY
CULTIVATING SOMETHING.
THEY WERE BOTH REGULAR
IN BEING GAY THERE.

[They vocalize together in close harmony.]

AH
AH!!

GEORGINE:

AH!

HELEN:

HA-HA-HA!

GEORGINE:

AH!

HELEN:

HA-HA-HA!

BOTH:

HA!

HELEN:

HELEN FURR WAS GAY THERE,
SHE WAS GAYER AND GAYER THERE
AND REALLY
SHE WAS JUST GAY THERE,
SHE WAS GAYER AND GAYER THERE,
THAT IS TO SAY
SHE FOUND WAYS OF BEING GAY THERE
SHE WAS GAY THERE,
ALWAYS SHE WAS GAY THERE.

[*They vocalize together in close harmony.*]

GEORGINE:

AH!

HELEN:

HA-HA-HA!

GEORGINE:

AH!

HELEN:

HA-HA-HA!

BOTH:

HA!

HELEN AND GEORGINE:

THEY WERE QUITE REGULARLY GAY THERE,
HELEN FURR AND GEORGINE SKEENE
THEY WERE REGULARLY GAY
THERE WHERE THEY WERE GAY.
THEY WERE VERY REGULARLY GAY.

[*They vocalize together in close harmony.*]

AH
AH!!

AH
AH
REGULARLY GAY.

[*The Three Young Men, as sailors,
are seated at a round table.
Young Gertrude and Alice observe the scene.
Gertrude plays bartender.*]

YOUNG GERTRUDE
[*speaking*]:

There were some dark and heavy men there then.

ALICE:

There were some who were not so heavy and some
who were not so dark.

YOUNG GERTRUDE AND ALICE:

Helen Furr and Georgine Skeene went regularly
with them.

YOUNG GERTRUDE:

They went with them regularly went with them.

ALICE:

They were regular then,

YOUNG GERTRUDE:

they were gay then,

ALICE:

they were where they wanted to be then where it was
gay to be then,

YOUNG GERTRUDE AND ALICE:

they were regularly gay then.

[*The three young sailors are
called Guy, Paul, and John.
They lift their glasses.*]

SAILORS (GUY, PAUL, AND JOHN)
[*singing*]:

SOME TIMES MEN ARE KISSING.
MEN ARE SOMETIMES KISSING
AND SOMETIMES DRINKING.
MEN ARE SOMETIMES KISSING ONE ANOTHER
AND SOMETIMES THEN
THERE ARE THREE OF THEM

AND ONE OF THEM IS TALKING
AND TWO OF THEM ARE KISSING
AND BOTH OF THEM,
BOTH OF THE TWO OF THEM
WHO ARE KISSING,
ARE HAVING THEIR EYES LARGE THEN
WITH THEIR BEING TEARS

GUY:

IN THEM . . .

PAUL AND JOHN
[*overlapping*]:

SOMETIMES MEN ARE DRINKING
AND ARE LOVING

GUY:

AND ONE OF THEM IS TALKING

PAUL AND JOHN:

AND TWO OF THEM ARE FIGHTING

PAUL:

AND ONE OF THE TWO OF THEM
IS WINNING ENOUGH

PAUL AND JOHN:

SO THAT THEY ARE THEN
HAVING LOVING IN THEM
AND ARE TELLING EACH OTHER
EVERYTHING.
ANYTHING.

PAUL:

ONE OF THEM IS LISTENING
TO ONE OTHER ONE.

GUY:

ONE OF THEM IS LISTENING
TO TWO OF THEM

JOHN:

ONE IS NOT LISTENING TO THEM
AN HE IS HAVING TEARS THEN
TEARS IN EMOTION

GUY, PAUL, AND JOHN:

AND THEY ARE ALL THREE THEN
DRINKING
AND TELLING EACH OTHER
EVERYTHING.

[*John walks away from the table.*
Paul buries his head in his hands.]

JOHN:

ONE OF THEM IS THEN
LARGE WITH THIS THING
QUITE LARGE WITH HAVING
TEARS ON HIM.

[*Paul fills his glass. John turns to go.*
Guy is looking at Paul.
Paul drinks slowly.]

JOHN:

THE LARGE ONE
WAS A LARGE ONE
AND WAS LEAVING

[*Slowly Guy approaches Paul.*
Paul finishes his drink
and looks up at Guy.]

JOHN:

WHEN NO ONE
WAS KNOWING THIS THING
WAS KNOWING
THAT HE WAS LEAVING.

[*John turns to see Guy and Paul dancing slowly.*]

JOHN:

WHEN NO ONE
WAS KNOWING THIS THING
WAS KNOWING
THAT HE WAS LEAVING.

ALICE
[*speaking*]:

Georgine Skeene went away to stay two months
with her brother.

YOUNG GERTRUDE
[*speaking*]:

Helen Furr stayed there where they had been regularly
living the two of them and she would then certainly
not be lonesome, she would go on being gay. She did
go on being gay. She was not any more gay but she
was gay longer every day than they had been being
gay when they were together being gay. She was gay
then quite exactly the same way.

[*Guy and Paul and John
dance slowly with
Young Gertrude,
Alice, and Georgine.
Helen is alone.
Gertrude observes her.*]

GERTRUDE:

She was not lonesome then, she was not at all feeling
any need of having Georgine Skeene. She was not
astonished at this thing. She would have been a little
astonished by this thing but she knew she was not
astonished at anything and so she was not astonished
at this thing not astonished at not feeling any need
of having Georgine Skeene.

[*singing a gentle habanero in tight harmony*]:

EACH ONE OF THE THREE OF THEM
WAS SUCH A ONE,
ONE THEY WERE THEN.
EACH ONE OF THEM
OF THE THREE OF THEM
MEANT SOMETHING
BY BEING SUCH A ONE.
EACH ONE OF THE THREE OF THEM
WAS SUCH A ONE,
ONE DRINKING AND TALKING AND LOVING.
EACH ONE OF THEM,
EACH ONE OF THE THREE OF THEM
HAD BEEN ONE DRINKING
WITH THE OTHER ONE
LOVING ONE OF THE THREE OF THEM,
LOVING TWO OF THE THREE OF THEM,
LOVING ALL THREE OF THEM,
KISSING ONE OF THEM,
CRYING SOME THEN.
EACH ONE OF THE THREE OF THEM
WERE SUCH ONES.
EACH ONE OF THE THREE OF THEM
MEANT SOMETHING
AS BEING SUCH A ONE.

YOUNG GERTRUDE AND ALICE
[speaking]:

They did not live together then Helen Furr and
Georgine Skeene.

[Georgine pins her hat
with a hat pin.]

GERTRUDE:

Helen Furr lived there the longer where they had
been living regularly together.

[Helen and Georgine
face each other.]

GERTRUDE, YOUNG GERTRUDE,
AND ALICE:

Then neither of them were living there any
longer.

HELEN

[singing]:

HELEN FURR WAS LIVING SOMEWHERE ELSE THEN
AND TELLING SOME ABOUT BEING GAY
AND SHE WAS GAY THEN
AND SHE WAS LIVING QUITE REGULARLY THEN.
SHE WAS REGULARLY GAY THEN.
SHE WAS QUITE REGULAR
IN BEING GAY THEN.
SHE REMEMBERED
ALL THE LITTLE WAYS
OF BEING GAY.
HMM . . .
SHE USED
ALL THE LITTLE WAYS
OF BEING GAY.

JOHN

[singing]:

HE WAS A LARGE ONE
IN REMEMBERING
THAT HE WAS NOT MEETING
ANY ONE WHO HAD BEEN.
HE WAS A LARGE ONE
IN REMEMBERING
THAT HE MIGHT BE MEETING

SOME ONE
WHO WAS FILLING SOMETHING.
HE WAS A LARGE ONE
IN BEING CRYING.
HMM . . .
HE WAS A LARGE ONE .
HE WAS REMEMBERING SOMETHING
IN BEING A LARGE ONE.
HE WAS REMEMBERING
BEING SUCH A ONE.

HELEN
[*overlapping*]:

SHE REMEMBERED
ALL THE LITTLE WAYS
OF BEING GAY.
SHE TOLD MANY THEN
THE WAY OF BEING GAY.
SHE WAS LIVING VERY WELL,
SHE WAS GAY THEN,
SHE WENT ON LIVING THEN,
SHE WAS REGULAR IN BEING GAY,
SHE WAS ALWAYS LIVING VERY WELL
AND WAS GAY VERY WELL . . .

JOHN
[*overlapping*]:

HE WAS REMEMBERING
THAT HE HAD MEANING

HELEN
[*overlapping*]:

AND WAS TELLING
ABOUT LITTLE WAYS
ONE COULD BE LEARNING
TO USE

HE WAS REMEMBERING
AGAIN AND AGAIN

IN BEING GAY

AND LATER WAS TELLING
   THEM

THAT HE WAS
SUCH A ONE

THAT SHE WAS
SUCH A ONE

SUCH A ONE

HE WAS SUCH A ONE

SUCH A ONE

QUITE OFTEN,
TELLING THEM

AND HE WAS REMEMBERING

AGAIN AND AGAIN.
AND AGAIN AND AGAIN.
AND AGAIN.

AGAIN AND AGAIN.
AND AGAIN AND AGAIN
AND AGAIN.

YOUNG GERTRUDE
[*speaking*]:

Perhaps no one ever gets a complete history of any one. This is very discouraging thinking. I am very sad now in this feeling. Always, hearing something, gives to some a sad feeling of realizing everything they have not been hearing and that they are not knowing and perhaps they can never have really in them the complete history of any one.

GERTRUDE
[*speaking*]:

I was all unhappy in this writing. I was nervous and driving and unhappy in it.

CHORUS
[*singing*]:

LOVING REPEATING IS ONE WAY OF BEING

YOUNG GERTRUDE
[*speaking*]:

There are so many complicated kinds of them.

CHORUS:

REPEATING IS ALWAYS IN ALL OF THEM.

YOUNG GERTRUDE:

So many ways of mixing, disguising, complicated
using of their natures in many of them,

CHORUS:

REPEATING IN THEM COMES OUT OF THEM.
SLOWLY . . .

YOUNG GERTRUDE
[*overlapping*]:

So complicated that mostly it is confusing to me
who know it of them . . .

CHORUS:

MAKING CLEAR TO ANYONE THAT
LOOKS CLOSELY AT THEM . . .

YOUNG GERTRUDE:

. . . always it is confusing.

GERTRUDE:

Being in men and women . . . is like a substance,
in some it is solid and sensitive all through it to
stimulation, in some almost wooden, in some muddy
and engulfing, in some thin almost like gruel, in some
solid in some parts and in other parts liquid, in some
with holes like air—holes in it, in some a thin layer
of it, in some hardened and cracked all through it.

Being is not an earthy kind of substance but a pulpy
not dust not dirt but a more mixed up substance, it
can be slimy, gelatinous, gluey, white opaquy kind of
thing and it can be white and vibrant, and clear and
heated and this is all not very clear to me . . .

CHORUS:

SLOWLY MAKING CLEAR TO ANYONE . . .

GERTRUDE:

. . . not very clear to me at all.

YOUNG GERTRUDE:

I have been heavy and have had much selecting. I saw
a star which was low. It was so low it twinkled.

YOUNG ALICE AND GERTRUDE
[*singing*]:

LIFTING BELLY IS SO NEAR
LIFTING BELLY IS SO DEAR
LIFTING BELLY ALL AROUND.
LIFTING BELLY MAKES A SOUND.
KEEP STILL.
MMM. KEEP STILL.
LIFTING BELLY IS A SUCCESS.
SO IS TENDERNESS.
LIFTING BELLY IS KIND AND GOOD
AND BEAUTIFUL.

ALICE:

BEAUTIFUL

BOTH:

LIFTING BELLY IS SUCH A REASON.
LIFTING BELLY IS SUCH A REASON.

ALICE:

WHY DO I SAY BENCH.

YOUNG GERTRUDE:

BECAUSE IT IS LAUGHABLE.

ALICE:

LIFTING BELLY IS SO DROLL.

YOUNG GERTRUDE:

ARE YOU THERE.

ALICE:

LIFTING BELLY.

YOUNG GERTRUDE:

WHAT DO I SAY.

ALICE:

PUSSY HOW PRETTY YOU ARE.

BOTH:

PUSSY HOW PRETTY YOU ARE.
LIFTING BELLY IS SO STRONG
LIFTING BELLY TOGETHER
LIFTING BELLY OH YES
LIFTING BELLY.
OH YES.

[*Gertrude walks slowly to the lectern.*]

GERTRUDE
[*speaking*]:

This is a picture of lifting belly having a cow . . .

CHORUS:

COME AND SING.
LIFTING BELLY.
I SING LIFTING BELLY

GERTRUDE
[speaking]:

I say lifting belly and then I say lifting belly and
Caesars. I say lifting belly gently and Caesars gently. I
say lifting belly again and Caesars again. I say lifting
belly and I say Caesars and I say lifting belly Caesars
and cow come out. I say lifting belly and Caesars and
cow come out.

[Alice is revealed as an old woman.]

CHORUS
[singing]:

HERE IS A BUN FOR MY BUNNY.
EVERY LITTLE BUN IS OF HONEY.
ON THE LITTLE BUN IS MY ONEY.
MY LITTLE BUN IS SO FUNNY.
 SWEET LITTLE BUN FOR MY MONEY.
DEAR LITTLE BUN I'M HER SUNNY
SWEET LITTLE BUN
DEAR LITTLE BUN
GOOD LITTLE BUN
FOR MY BUNNY.
LIFTING BELLY EXACTLY.
WHY CAN LIFTING BELLY PLEASE ME.

LIFTING BELLY CAN PLEASE ME
BECAUSE IT IS AN OCCUPATION
I ENJOY.
ROSE IS A ROSE IS A ROSE
IS A ROSE
IS A ROSE.

[*Gertrude stands alone in a shaft of light.*]

GERTRUDE:

Well like it or not everybody has to do something
to fill the time. After all human beings have to live
dogs too so as not to know that time is passing, that
is the whole business of living to go on so they will
not know that time is passing, that is why they get
drunk that is why they like to go to war during a war
there is the most complete absence of the sense that
time is passing a year of war lasts so much longer
than any other year. After all that is what life is
and that is the reason there is no Utopia, little or
big young or old dog or man everybody wants
every minute so filled that they are not conscious
of that minute passing. It's just as well they do not
think about it you have to be a genius to live in it
and know it to exist in it and and express it to
accept it and deny it by creating it . . .

[*Alice stands near Gertrude at the lectern.*]

Anyway, I began to wonder if it was possible to describe the way every possible kind of human being acted and felt in relation with any other kind of human being and I thought if this could be done it would make A Long Gay Book. I began A Long Gay Book and it was to describe not only every possible kind of human being, but every possible kind of pairs of human beings and every possible threes and fours and fives of human beings and every possible crowds of human beings. And I was going to do it as A Long Gay Book and that was in a kind of way to go on and to keep going on and to go on before and it began in this way . . .

ALICE AS AN OLDER WOMAN
[*singing*]:

I SPY A FLY.
IT WAS A BEE.
YOU ARE MY HONEY HONEY SUCKLE.
I AM YOUR BEE.

[*Gertrude turns from lectern and Alice helps her on with her coat. Alice buttons the coat tenderly.*]

GERTRUDE

[*to Alice*]:

It is hard to go on when you are nearly there but
not nearly enough to hurry up to get there.

[*Gertrude caresses Alice's cheek.*]

CHORUS:

KISS MY LIPS SHE DID.
KISS MY LIPS AGAIN SHE DID.
KISS MY LIPS OVER AND OVER AGAIN . . .

[*Gertrude turns and walks into darkness.
Alice comes to the lectern.
The Chorus hums under the following.*]

ALICE

[*speaking*]:

By this time Gertrude Stein was in a sad state of
indecision and worry. I sat next to her and she said
to me early in the afternoon, what is the answer? I
was silent. In that case, she said, what is the question?

Then the whole afternoon was troubled, confused and very uncertain, and later in the afternoon they took her away on a wheeled stretcher to the operating room and I never saw her again.

[*Alice turns and walks slowly away,
lighting a cigarette as she goes.*]

CHORUS:

YOU ARE MY HONEY HONEY SUCKLE.
I AM YOUR BEE.

[*Lights fade to darkness.*]

Gertrude Stein (Cindy Gold, left) stands by
as Young Gertrude (Christine Mild)
sings, "I spy a fly."

Gertrude Stein (Cindy Gold) narrates as
Georgine Skeene (Harriet Nzinga Plumpp) and
Helen Furr (Cristen Paige) propel Young Gertrude
(Christine Mild) and Alice B. Toklas (Jenny Powers)
around the stage on gliding chairs.

The entire company (Cristen Paige, Jenny Powers,
Bernie Yvon, Cindy Gold, Zach Ford,
Harriet Nzinga Plumpp, Christine Mild, and
Travis Turner) sings, "On the fifteenth of October."

Helen Furr (Cristen Paige, left) and
Georgine Skeene (Harriet Nzinga Plumpp)
sing, "They were very regularly gay."

*The Two Young Women (Harriet Nzinga Plumpp
and Cristen Paige) look on in the background as the
Three Young Men (Zach Ford, Bernie Yvon, and Travis Turner)
morph into drinking and kissing sailors.*

Alice B. Toklas (Jenny Powers) passionately recites
"Lifting Belly" to Young Gertrude (Christine Mild)
in the presence of Gertrude Stein (Cindy Gold).

ABOUT THE PLAYWRIGHT

Frank Galati is a playwright, director, and actor. He was nominated for a Tony Award for directing the Broadway musical *Ragtime,* with music by Stephen Flaherty and lyrics by Lynn Aherns. He received two Tony Awards for his adaptation and direction of *The Grapes of Wrath.* Galati is a member of the Steppenwolf Theatre Ensemble and a professor emeritus at Northwestern University. In 2000, he was inducted into the American Academy of Arts and Sciences.